Break Free and Soar: Letting Go of Fear, Anxiety, and Depression

Wynette Turner

Break Free and Soar: Letting Go of Fear, Anxiety, and Depression

Dedications

This book is dedicated to my Lord and Savior, Jesus Christ. God, I thank you so much for your patience, love, and for never giving up on me. This book is written out of obedience to you, Lord Jesus. We did this together, and I feel so blessed to have your Holy Spirit operating so strong in my life. From the day you told me to write and I said yes, you have divinely orchestrated every step. I ask that you bless every hand that touches this book and that the reader will break free and soar in every aspect of life. You gave me the wisdom and discernment throughout this entire process and for that alone, I say thank you Jesus!

Contents

Acknowledgments

To my wonderful husband Derrick, my high school sweetheart, thank you so much for your continuous love and support throughout this entire process. You have been there for me from the beginning. You encouraged me to keep going no matter what comes my way. I love you honey!

To my children, Michael and Jasmine, I love you more than anything. You both give my life so much meaning and purpose. Thank you for encouraging me to get this book done and believing in me. I love you both!

To my parents, Johnny and Eva DiBartolo, words cannot express my love for you both. I owe you so much, and I thank you from the bottom of my heart for raising me with strong knowledge in the Word of God! Thank you for your many sacrifices so that I can be where I am today. I will continue to make you proud. I love you, Mom and Dad!

To my big brother, Johnny DiBartolo III, his wife Dwanell, and their children Johnny and Trinity.

Thank you for the words of wisdom and advice given to me throughout my life, and letting me know that I have what it takes to accomplish anything in life. I love you all.

To Bishop Hargrave and my Gospel Tabernacle church family. Thank you Bishop for your life-changing sermons and for encouraging me to take action and commit to the work of the Lord.

To Marie LaGarde, thank you and my mama for being the first ones to read my unedited copy and make those initial corrections. You took the time to talk with me and encourage me to keep going and to get it done.

To my supporters, when you found out that I was writing a book, you continued to encourage and push me along and reminded me that others are waiting for my story!

Introduction

Fear! Anxiety! Stress! Depression! These negative emotions gripped me for so long. Somewhere along the way, I was silenced and went into hiding. I don't mean literally, I mean spiritually. I ran from the power that was lying dormant in me. I graduated from high school, college, then graduate school feeling so great and enthused about life. I had it all planned out.

I kept telling myself I have so much to say, but I felt fear of even talking about my pain. I am a dance minister, and for years I stopped dancing due to depression because my life wasn't going the way I planned. I got married at 27 and was silently suffering for years due to a lack of emotional connection. After 10 years of marriage, I was divorced at the age of 37. I was devastated, broken, and empty. I looked good on the outside but on the inside, I was embarrassed and ashamed that my marriage had ended. We had adopted two children, and here I was a single mom. I felt sorry for myself and my kids. They were both removed from their birth families and now experiencing more devastation in losing their adoptive father.

I wondered, where do I go from here? How do I parent these two beautiful children I chose to adopt? How would I be able to make the right decisions? How would I continue to financially provide for them? I have to admit that although I learned to put on a brave face, I was honestly scared. I was over 1000 miles away from home in New Orleans, where my parents reside. I considered selling my home and moving back to New Orleans so my parents could help me raise my children. I am a full-time elementary school counselor, and I even began looking for a job in different parts of Louisiana. My parents were both open and very supportive of us moving home. My main hesitation was finding the right care for my daughter who has a liver condition called biliary atresia. She was already receiving excellent care from the UNC medical team. I didn't want to risk her healthcare due to all that was already going on and the drastic changes that were taking place. I was also unsure about uprooting my son because he loved the school he was attending and had already begun making friends. I shared this idea with my parents and of course, they supported me. They even suggested that instead of moving to New Orleans, they would come and stay with me for 3-4 weeks at a time to help me out. I had so much anxiety over trying to make the right decision because two precious lives were depending on me, and I didn't want to mess up. The main struggle for me has always been this fear of making mistakes due to wrong decisions. My father reminded me that it's okay to make mistakes and once you make a decision, you accept the consequences — whatever that may be — and to move on and keep pushing forward. I knew he was correct but internally, I had lots of anxiety in that area. In my mind, I was going back and forth about whether my decision was the best one. Well, I decided to stay in North Carolina and parent my children as a single mom with the help of my parents when they visited! I was still silently suffering.

So many women are suffering in silence for various reasons. So many women are depressed but they keep it bottled up. Many women, particularly Black women, have been taught to be strong and just handle it. The truth is, we are suffering in silence because we are afraid to talk about the fact that we are having mental health issues. We have to be able to talk about it. Most of all, we have to know we are not alone. I pray a special anointing over this book and over the words being printed in this book. I thank God for allowing me to pour out my heart, and I pray that I can help others break free and truly soar. My only regret is that I did not write this book sooner because I could have been free a long time ago, and I could have helped free others sooner. However, I know that God's timing is perfect and that I am exactly where I need to be.

Chapter 1

It is not easy to break free. Once you decide to open up and express your inner feelings, you release anxieties and you notice a difference in how you feel. When you first start, it will be hard because you are asking God to strip away things from you that your flesh may want to keep because it feels good. Often, we become complacent in our comfort zones.

When you say yes to God, you begin the process of making life changes while having past hurts, guilt, regrets, and negative vibes burned off of you. I promise you will feel 100% better because you will know you are in the will of God, and that is the best place to be in your life.

When I found the ministry of dance, I got my fire back. This was an excellent way to serve God and put some of my gifts and talents to use. I am living solely for God. I will do everything God tells me to do from now on. I will no longer be stagnant and frozen or afraid to step out on faith because the fear I carried for so long, did not serve me well at all.

I remember feeling anxious about going away to Wesleyan College in Macon, Georgia, eight hours away from my home in New Orleans. Even though a few friends from my high school attended college with me, I still felt alone at times. I had high expectations of myself and was under a lot of pressure to do well. I also attended an all African American, female junior and high school, so I was accustomed to learning in the atmosphere of African American ladies. I believe the pressure I was feeling was because Wesleyan was a predominantly White school, and even though it was all-female, I was not quite comfortable. I had to mentally prepare to work hard and find a way to be successful in college.

I chose psychology as my major. I sat in my first psychology class and I loved learning about the mind and body language of others. When it was time to prepare for my first psychology exam, I studied hard. On the day of the test, I felt ready. I was feeling anxious, but I still felt ready. I completed the test, turned it in, and moved on to my next class. A few days later I received the test back. I was devastated. I scored a 59. What? I just wanted to scream. On the way back to my dorm room I felt so bad, inadequate, and unequipped for college. I simply could not believe that I failed my first college exam. I called my parents and my brother, who was about six years older than me and also a pastor. I cried, fussed, and complained. I was beating myself up for deciding to attend a college nearly eight hours away from home. I blamed them as well. The truth is, I was so afraid to fail. My brother talked to me privately and asked me how I prepared for the test. I told him I studied nonstop for hours with no break. He told me to go back to my professor and ask him to teach me how to study and find out how future tests would be structured. I was reluctant to do this, but I took his advice. I left my dorm room and walked across the lawn to my professor's office. I was scared but determined to figure this out. I could not fail. I would not fail. I walked into his office and we talked. I expressed to him that I was very upset that I failed my first psychology test and I needed to know how to study. He also asked me how I studied and prepared for the test. When I explained to him how I did it, he said I had studied wrong. Of course, this was shocking to hear. He explained to me that I sent my brain into overload and I crammed too much in at one time. He advised me to take more breaks in between studying to allow my brain to process all of that information. Now, that information may seem very simple to you, but it was life-changing for me. When you are properly aligned to receive and make necessary changes and corrections, amazing things will happen. I applied all the tips and nuggets he shared with me and something amazing happened. On the next exam, I scored a high B. After that for the rest of my college days, I made mostly A's, including tests in other subjects. I graduated from Wesleyan College with a 3.8 GPA. To God be the glory! I knew even though I struggled with anxiety, I was determined not to allow it to get in my way. I was 18 years old and felt so proud of myself for not allowing fear and anxiety to stop me. When you desire to win, you will not let anything stop you from achieving that goal. It is so easy to allow fear to stop you, but you have the POWER to make up your mind that no matter what, you will succeed. You may have setbacks in life, and you may even fall off the wagon, but please get back up again and keep going!

The biggest lesson I have learned is that fear and anxiety comes from a lack of self-confidence, self-esteem, and courage.

"You get in life what you have the courage to ask for."- Oprah Winfrey

Courage is the strength to keep going even when you are afraid. You must do it anyway. I do not claim to have arrived, but I will say I am growing and getting better every day. I am now aware of my thoughts, feelings, and actions. Self-awareness is powerful, and once you have it, you will live on another level in your life! I realized I had to align myself with the right people and the right mentors who would push me to keep going. Alignment is defined as an arrangement in a straight line or correct or appropriate relative positions of agreement. It was time for me to be catapulted into new levels of myself. However, reaching new levels must first happen in your mind and your heart. New levels mean new lessons, new connections, new expectations, and lots of continual growth! This is why alignment is so very important. I am working daily on my goals and the assignment God has given to me, and I am learning to trust the process.

"When you want to succeed as bad as you want to breathe, then you will be successful." -Eric Thomas

On February 26, 2018, I remarried. Derrick and I are both from New Orleans, and he was my high school sweetheart. I feel so blessed that after being single for three years, God blessed me with such a wonderful man who is also my best friend. On March 22, 2018, we were discussing home improvements. He told me time and time again the house was too dark, and it needed more light. He told me it was time to redecorate.

Old curtains and old furniture needed to be removed. It was time for a fresh start. I got up from the table and walked over to the window and began taking down the dining room curtain. As soon as those curtains were down, I felt a shift in the spirit. It was like a weight had been lifted off of me. I cried and thanked God. My husband looked at me in shock because I suddenly burst into tears over curtains. He understood later that sudden change can cause anxiety for me, which is why I procrastinated. At that moment, I felt as if I went to a new level in God! I felt as if Jesus had washed away the wounds from my past. I walked into my living room and removed those curtains as well. The room was so much brighter, and my vision was so much clearer.

I thought about other women and how symbolic it is for them to take down their curtains as well. Curtains symbolized the bondages and pains of the past. For me, those curtains were fear, anxiety, stress, and bondage.

Ask yourself:

What's holding you back?

What's blocking you from your NEXT blessing?

What is holding you back from being truly delivered and set free?

In the Waiting

After releasing some pains and past hurts to God, it was time to wait and see what God wanted me to do next. Vicky Yohe recorded a song called "In the Waiting." I love that song. It teaches me about the real meaning of the word *patience*. Webster dictionary defines *patience* as the capacity to accept or tolerate delay; being patient has to become a habit to develop patience. The two words to stand out to me are *capacity* and *habit*. I have learned when God calls you to wait, it is because He believes you have the capacity or the innate drive to wait. It's almost as if He wants it to become a habit for me to be patient yet rejoicing while I wait. While we wait on that blessing or promise from God, He wants us to sing and dance. Rejoice ahead of time believing and knowing He will bring it to pass. Is there anything too hard for the Lord? Here are some great questions to ask yourself while you are "In the Waiting" phase of your life. I have asked myself these same questions too.

1. Am I grumbling and complaining about waiting?
2. What is God trying to tell me and through me while I'm waiting?
3. Is my attitude pleasing God while I'm "In the Waiting"?
4. Are you still praying faithfully, or has your faith diminished because God is taking a long time to answer or move the way you think He should?
5. Do you still believe in His promises that He will come through for you?
6. Do you realize God's timing is not your time?

These are some questions to think about while you are waiting on God. I want to encourage you to hold on and never give up on God. As long as your desires line up with God's desires, He will see you through. I am believing God with you. When you have a moment, listen to the beautiful song called "In the Waiting" by Vicki Yohe!

Even though I don't always understand why I go through certain trials, I'm so thankful I know the importance of obedience to God! One thing I know for sure is that obedience WILL deliver you to your next blessing. I am learning to stop comparing myself, my children, or my family to anyone else because it will certainly steal your joy and happiness.

"Do not conform to this world but be ye transformed by the renewing of your mind"- Romans 12:2

Chapter 2

The Gift of Adoption: My Son

Eight days before my son came into our family, I received a prophetic word from Marsha Burns. It said "Refuse to allow your current challenges to overwhelm you. Stay calm and take life one bite at a time. Trust me to lead you one step at a time. You will need the wisdom to know how to proceed. So you must ask and wait for my download, says the Lord for I will indeed show you what to do next. Stress will swallow you up if you allow uncertainty and fear to rule over you. Be strong and stay steady." May 8, 2006.

On May 8, 2008, we fostered and then adopted our son. He came to our home when he was 21 months. When we met him at our home, he walked in and I was immediately drawn to him. He was so adorable, and he instantly connected with us. When I finally held him in my arms, he fell asleep within 10 minutes. I knew at that moment he was ours to love. It was such a blessing to bond with him so quickly and naturally. I have always told my son that he was truly born in my heart.

He truly loved to eat, and in the very first few months, he was always checking to see if we had more food. Eventually, he became comfortable in our home and knew there would always be food available to him. He couldn't talk, so I began teaching him different words and sounds. I remember his first word was "juice" because that was what he wanted to drink. Shortly after that, he began to say mama and then daddy.

As time went on, our boy began forming letters, sounds, then words. Then all of a sudden, he blurted out his first sentence, "MOMMY, I SEE THE MOON!" I was so proud of him.

He was such a driven child that I knew with the proper tools, support, and guidance, he would be successful in life. When he started kindergarten, he received several reading and math awards. He beat all the odds stacked against him. He continues to thrive and grow in school. At the early age of five, I noticed his athletic gift when we would throw a ball back and forth to each other. He received a Little Tykes basketball goal and his cute little face just lit up. I signed him up to take lessons at our local recreational center, and as I watched him try out and play with his team, I knew God had blessed him with a special gift. I decided to invest in his basketball career, and this is the path my husband and I are on now.

My son is now a 13-year-old young man who is thriving in every area of his life. He is doing very well in school. He loves to read, and it is a joy to see him engaged in a great book. He is also a very good basketball player on his school and AAU team. I enjoy watching him play because he plays with such character, hustle, heart, and he is a team player. He is a very respectful young man, and my husband and I are diligently teaching him everything he needs to be successful in life. Derrick is doing an amazing job raising him to grow into the man God is calling our son to be. He has this inner strength in him that I admire. He is a great friend to others, and he is a leader. I love that he stands up for what is right. He loves helping and encouraging little kids, and they love being around him too. As I write this book, I feel so excited about all the things my young man will accomplish! I love Michael so much, and every day, I feel so blessed to be his mom.

The Gift of Adoption: My Daughter

My daughter has a different story. I met this beautiful baby while she was in the hospital. At the age of two months, our princess was diagnosed by her doctors with a rare, incurable liver condition called biliary atresia. I found out right before I was ready to take her home. I panicked and did not know if I could handle it. She takes medication two times a day and gets bloodwork done every three months to check her levels. This has always been very traumatic for her, but she is a trooper and gets through it with courage and prayer. My girl has been hospitalized five times before the age of four. It is fitting to say that she is one courageous little girl. She has a spunky personality and is considered by many to be a little diva! She is now in second grade and is ready to take on the world despite her academic struggles. She wants to own a hair and nail salon when she grows up.

September 18, 2012 was the day we brought our little blessing home. It changed my life forever! I thought I was saving her but in reality, she was saving me! I received the phone call from social services saying they had a baby who needed a home. At nine months old, she was 13 pounds and extremely malnourished. I was immediately drawn to her because I knew I could easily help her become well-nourished.

My son who was five at the time came with me to meet this precious baby! As soon as I walked up to the desk, I told the nurse who I was looking for. When we arrived, she was in the arms of one of the nurses. I walked up to the two of them, and she quickly looked at me. Another nurse said it may be hard for her to come to me because she had gotten so attached to them. I opened up my arms to her and she immediately came to me and grabbed my name tag off of my shirt. It was such a precious moment, and I think she surprised all of them. I bonded with her for five hours in her hospital room. My son and I enjoyed her so much, as we knew that she was special.

My ex-husband came to the hospital and he connected with this beautiful baby as well. Everything was going well, and I was feeling very excited and confident about caring for this baby. Around 5 o'clock, the doctor came in and thanked us for taking in our precious baby despite her liver disease. I immediately went into a panic attack. I quietly excused myself and went to the bathroom. LIVER DISEASE!!! WHAT???? I couldn't believe what I heard. I had bonded and connected with her for five hours and thought she was just malnourished. However, we discovered fairly quickly that it wasn't just neglect and malnourishment, it was a serious health condition. As a result, so many thoughts of doubt and fear ran through my head. I didn't know how we could do this. How could I mother her? Was I even capable of managing this condition enough to keep her healthy and alive? However, it was too late to turn back now. Our hearts had already intertwined. I came out of the bathroom and pretended that everything was okay. On the inside, I was a complete mess. I asked the doctor the details about this liver condition. He explained to me that there was a possibility that this baby would need a liver transplant at some point in her life, but she could still live a normal healthy life. My heart was racing so fast. I was in shock, and I was so afraid. I began to doubt my decision for a moment. Was I going to do her more harm because I had no experience in this area? When we took her home, my bedroom looked like a mini-hospital. She was sent home with a feeding tube through her nose.

The liver condition is called biliary atresia. It is defined as a rare disease of the liver and bile ducts that occur in infants. Symptoms of this disease appear to develop about two to eight weeks after birth. Cells within the liver produce liquid bile and bile that helps to digest fat.

When she was two months, she had surgery for biliary atresia. It's called the Kasai procedure. During the surgery, the surgeon removes any problem bile ducts outside the liver. The small intestine is then attached to the liver. It won't work if the bile ducts inside the child's liver are damaged or missing. Well, I am happy to say that the surgery worked well for her, and it was a complete success. To maintain her health, she takes two medications twice a day as well as vitamins. Also, every six months she has to have bloodwork done to check her levels. As you can imagine, this is very traumatizing for her. It's hard for me as her mom to see her so upset. During the drive to the lab, I encourage her along the way and reassure her that I will be with her every step of the way. I remember a time when she encouraged herself and talked herself through it. She was six years old saying, "Okay God, I can do this." Then she would say, "But why God?" Then back to, "Okay, I got this!" In those moments, I realized all over again that God placed a little trooper in my life who is so brave even through the tears. To God be the glory!

Before leaving the hospital, the doctor shared with me she was on a feeding tube because she was not comfortable taking a bottle. I asked the doctor what she and I could do to help her become comfortable so I could increase her weight. When he said it was between me and her (meaning it depended on how well she bonded and connected with me) I immediately looked into her eyes and told this precious baby that together we were going to do this.

She was very attached to her Gumdrop pacifier. It was her absolute favorite. The doctor also shared with me that while in the hospital, my girl was on four different medications twice a day to keep her liver functioning. This broke my heart so much. Four medications? This was way too much for my baby to take every day. Remember, she was only nine months and 13 pounds when I brought her home.

Can you imagine for a moment how overwhelmed I had become? We had already adopted a beautiful boy. I felt so much pressure as a mom to continue to meet all of his needs (which were non-medical) while meeting her serious medical needs. Despite my fears and anxieties, we signed all the necessary discharge papers so my baby could leave the hospital and go to her new home.

I safely and securely buckled her in the backseat of my car. As I drove away from the hospital, I cried silently. I immediately called my friend Elizabeth, who is more like a sister to me, and I cried even more. She talked to me until I got home and encouraged me that I was fully capable of raising her and that God will take care of us.

When I arrived home, my ex-husband set up her feeding tube machine in the bedroom so we could keep a close watch on her. I stayed up all night and watched her sleep. I was scared so of course, I did what I do best and that is to pray. I prayed and laid hands over her. Would you believe that very next day in the afternoon, Jazzy pulled the feeding tube out of her nose? I was blown away by her and by God. It was almost as if she looked at me and said: "Let's Do This!!!" So we did!!!!

I had to figure out a way for her to gain weight because she was also malnourished. She was a nine-month-old baby weighing only 13 pounds who decided to take her feeding tube out herself. She was showing me early on how determined and strong she was.

I had to teach her to trust me and to take the bottle so I could help increase her weight and get her healthy. She was so attached to her Gumdrop pacifier and would slightly shy away from the bottle, so I decided to put the bottle in the corner of her mouth while the pacifier was on the other side of her mouth. She was sucking on the pacifier and getting milk from her bottle at the same time. This may sound crazy, but it was all that I could think of to get her to not fear the bottle. Eventually, I removed the pacifier and she began taking a bottle for her feeding. Yes! Go Princess and Go Jesus!!!

The whole time during her feeding, I would look into her eyes and talk to her and let her know that the bottle was okay; the milk was good inside of this bottle. Eventually, she drank it as she looked me in the eye and built trust.

Another phase that I had to embrace was having nurses, a physical therapist, and the occupational therapist visit regularly. This was so out of my comfort zone, but I didn't care because I was focused on helping her gain weight.

Every day or every other day, a nurse would come into our home to check her weight to make sure she was responding to the formula. We found out she needed to relearn how to crawl and walk because she had learned incorrectly. We gave her physical therapy, and she wore this cute little brace on her foot. I remember the day she crawled up the stairs on her own using her strength. It was one of the most beautiful moments ever! Immediately, I knew this child was not here by accident. I knew God had His hand on her and that she was one determined, strong, driven child who will never give up on life.

Hospital Story

At the end of August 2015, she developed a fever that just would not go away. After a couple of days, I decided to take her to urgent care. While there, I was told she didn't look too good and that I should take her to UNC Hospital ER. I was so shocked and scared. God's timing is amazing. My parents had just flown in from New Orleans. At this time, I was a single woman and I was so thankful for my parents being there for me and my children. Please bear with me as I write this portion because it brings back painful memories of my daughter having to go through so much. I arrived at the hospital. While we sat in the ER, they rushed in swiftly and admitted her as quickly as possible. They drew blood and immediately became alarmed by the results. Her numbers were extremely high — in the 500 to 600 range — which meant that her liver was inflamed and infected. I am in tears as I write this because I remember when the doctor told me she would be hospitalized for 21 days and that she would need a PICC line. My anxiety level was so high. I was in shock and I felt scared. A PICC line is a thin, soft, long catheter (tube) that is inserted into a vein in the child's arm, leg, or neck. The tip of the catheter is positioned in a large vein that carries blood into the heart. The PICC line is used for long-term intravenous (IV) antibiotics, nutrition or medication and for blood draws.

This procedure required her to go under anesthesia. I walked down the hall on the way to her procedure, and I held her and just talked to her — letting my girl know everything would be alright, and I was right there for her. I assured her that I would never leave her. She looked up at me when she was on the table right before the medicine would take effect, putting her to sleep. The look she gave me was one that said *please get me out of here*. It was such a scary time for us all, and my heart was truly broken and sad that my baby girl was going through that.

The procedure took about an hour, but I was in another realm on another level. Initially, I didn't even reach out to Facebook people for prayer because I just didn't want anybody feeling sorry for her or any of us. Close friends and co-workers knew because I had to take off work. I also notified my pastor, and he along with several ministers came and prayed over my baby. That was a blessing. I truly thank God for my parents and other family members and close friends who came to the hospital as well.

My sweet boy was about seven at the time and didn't quite understand what was going on. He just knew that something was wrong. I did my best to keep him occupied and happy as possible, so he stayed at home with my dad during those three weeks while my mom and I stayed at the hospital. There were a couple of times I had to leave her because I had to go to work, but my mom stayed there with her every single day. She never left my daughter's side. The times when the nurses had to come and clean the area around the PICC line were rough, so scary, and tedious. She would cry in fear and panic, and I would lie in the bed with her and just hold her. This process took about five minutes or more, and it required two nurses to do it. The nurses had to move quickly because it was an open wound and they didn't want it to get infected.

She had about three different medications that were flowing through the tubes. To get her ALT, AST, and bilirubin numbers down, they had to give it to her in small amounts over the course of three long weeks. There were times she could be off the machine with the tube still in her arm. We enjoyed those moments of freedom because my parents and I would take her for a walk throughout the hospital. We also took her for a walk outside just to give her a sense of normalcy and a breath of fresh air. She was so happy and full of joy!

There were also times when the medicine was taking a toll on her body and she vomited a couple of times. I was not in the room when that happened, but my mom was right there for her. I believe God was sparing my mind and emotions because I was already trying to be strong for my daughter. I have to say she remained in good spirits the whole time. Jazzy handled everything like a champion; she was so strong and determined to come through in victory. My goal was to focus on being strong for her and her brother. I remember the way he embraced her after not seeing her for a few days. It was priceless and filled with so much love.

I wanted everyone at the hospital to know I was very serious about my daughter getting out of the hospital successfully. My girl is an overcomer, and it was time for her to be healed. After she developed a fever in her third and last week, I decided not to play any more games with the devil. I decided that enough was enough. When the doctors were contemplating putting her on the fourth medication, I said no more! The next day her fever broke. Yes!!! It BROKE!

About two days before she was to be discharged, she removed her PICC line out of her chest while she was sleeping. My mom was sleeping on the sofa, and I was sitting in a chair near her bed. I screamed and woke my mom and whoever was sleeping nearby. The nurses in the hallway heard me and ran into the room. You see, the PICC line was surgically implanted while my girl was under anesthesia and was supposed to be removed by the surgeon only. However, with the help of her angels, the PICC line was removed on the 20th day, and to all of our surprise, there was very little blood and no damage to her chest or heart. To God be the glory! All praises and honor belong to Jesus!

The movie *War Room* had come out, but I hadn't had a chance to see it. On a preview, there was a lady who was putting Scriptures on sticky notes in her prayer room. All of that came back to me and the anointing fell on me. At that moment, God 's Holy Spirit rushed over me. I went into the lobby and asked the nurses for Post-it Notes. I grabbed a Bible and began writing healing Scriptures. I sat in the lobby looking up every Scripture I could find on healing, and I wrote down one Scripture on each card until I had about 10 of them. I walked into her room and I taped the Scripture cards on the wall, over her bed, on the medical chart they came in and checked every morning, and on the inside and outside of the door of her room. I was ready for war, and I was ready to fight the enemy. I wanted everyone in the hospital to know that I am a child of God, a praying woman, and a praying mother. I prayed to God that He would take care of my baby girl, that He would heal her liver, and that we would never have to go back there again. Now according to the doctors, there is no cure for her condition, but according to my faith, God is a healer and He can do ANYTHING, and I DECLARE that she will live to tell about it. One thing my father told me was to have crazy, radical faith that doesn't make sense to anyone except those who have crazy faith too.

As I write this, I'm crying tears of thankfulness. I rarely talk about this, so getting it out now in this book is freedom and healing for me. I pray that it blesses you and so many others as well. That brings me to this day. My princess is doing very well. She is still taking her medication twice a day, but I KNOW she is healed. I believe God and his promises and that is what I am holding onto.

Both Mike and Jazzy have had to experience some emotional hardships. They both were separated from their biological families and then separated from their adoptive father due to my divorce. I have always struggled with the guilt of them having to experience so many major losses because it just doesn't seem fair. However, I serve an Almighty God who has His powerful hand on us. I thought I was changing their lives when I took them in and later adopted them, but the truth is, they have changed my life far more than they will ever know.

Breaking Free

Something in me began to awaken and rise up. It was the power and strength of God! It was the belief that I was anointed and equipped for this! I was equipped to mother these children whom God entrusted to me. It was that inner voice reassuring me that I was built for this and God had already prepared me for this. As I am writing this, I think of the song that the late Daryl Coley sang, "He's Preparing Me." This was exactly what God had done. All the years of praying and fasting were preparing me for this moment. It was on now!

He's Preparing Me!

Lyrics by the late Daryl Coley

He's preparing me for something

I cannot handle right now

He's making me ready

Just because He cares

He's providing me with what I'll need

To carry out the next matter in my life

Preparing me

He cares for me

Preparing me

For everything

That comes in my life

"To whom much is given much is required."-Luke 12:48

This means I have a duty and responsibility to share my gift and my story with others. It's so easy to sit on our gifts due to fear of what others may think, fear of failing, or sometimes fear of being successful. I wrote this book trusting and believing it will get into the hands of those whom God wanted to read it.

Chapter 3

We all learn in different ways! I am in the process of understanding learning disabilities such as dyslexia and processing disorders. Dyslexia is a general term for disorders that involve difficulty in learning to read or interpret words, letters, and other symbols, but that does not affect general intelligence. Dyslexia is a specific learning disability that is neurobiological in origin. It is characterized by difficulties with accurate and/or fluent word recognition and by poor spelling and decoding abilities. These difficulties typically result from a deficit in the phonological component of language that is often unexpected concerning other cognitive abilities and the provision of effective classroom instruction. Secondary consequences may include problems in reading comprehension and reduced reading experience that can impede the growth of vocabulary and background knowledge. This learning disability has affected my daughter and school is currently a struggle for her. She received extra services by being pulled out of her classroom for about three years. We are working hard every day to help her be successful. She is a hands-on learner. If you show her how to do it or another way that it can be done, with time and practice, she can do it. Stay tuned for my second book on the effects of learning disabilities on children and their families and how we are overcoming.

I was listening to a sermon by T.D. Jakes. Here is what he said:

* It takes courage to be different.
* It takes courage to be successful.
* It takes courage to stand out.
* It takes courage to be exceptional.
* It takes courage to be rich.
* It takes courage to educated.
* It takes courage to be knowledgeable.
* It takes courage to be exceptional.
* It takes courage to be wise.
* It takes courage to win.
* It takes courage to think outside the box.

No more fitting in! No more neutralizing myself, my gift, or my uniqueness just to fit in. It takes courage to face your fears. It took courage for me to adopt and mother two bloodlines. It takes courage to pursue your dreams not knowing if you will have enough money. It certainly takes courage to step out on faith. I have decided I am not wasting any more time on my fears. I refuse to let my fears cause me to disobey God and all of the things and assignments He has given me. I realized the longer I procrastinated on writing this book, the longer I kept others in bondage. Someone needs this book and needs to hear my story. God's timing is perfect, and he strategically places the right people in my path. You were chosen to read this book, and I pray whatever has you locked up or in bondage, you are FREE right now in the mighty Name of Jesus!

"And when the day of Pentecost was fully come, they were all with one accord in one place. And suddenly there came a sound from heaven as of a rushing mighty wind, and it filled all the house where they were sitting." -Acts 2:1-2

In this Scripture, it is clear that suddenly the atmosphere changed. When your atmosphere changes, you are now open to whatever God wants to do in your life. It's not going to be easy to change your atmosphere, and you may have to say goodbye to some negative and toxic people. You are not trying to hurt them. You have to be obedient to God. You have to get to YOUR next level.

No More Hiding

I had to move from fear to faith. There are so many things God told me to do, and I allowed fear to stop me. I got to a point in my life that I was tired of hiding, tired of being afraid, and tired of keeping my story to myself. I was tired of comparing myself to others. I knew God had instilled a gift in me, and I knew God had anointed me to do great things. I became angry at the enemy but more so angry at myself for allowing the enemy to steal my joy, to steal my dreams, to diminish my goals, and to make me think that due to my anxiety and my fears, I wasn't even qualified to say anything or to try to help other people.

We have to be careful not to wait until we have it all together before we help others. It's okay to be in the process. It's okay to grow while you're helping others because, at some point, your time will come where you will accomplish that goal. Eventually, with much prayer and faith, you will get healing. You have to keep going.

What Does It Mean to Surrender to God?

Webster defines *surrender* as the action of yielding one's person or giving up the possession of something, especially into the power of another.

It is imperative to spend quality time with Jesus. Carve out some time in your day every day, even if it's just a few minutes to stop and read the word and pray. As you commit to this type of lifestyle, the time you spend with Jesus will increase more and more.

If you have seen the movie *War Room*, do you remember the main character, the wife who initially was suggested by Clara to spend time with Jesus? Initially, the wife was uncomfortable in her prayer room closet, but it didn't take very long before she was seeking and longing for more of God. Eventually, she was basking in His glory.

Depression is Real but Can Be Managed

According to the National Institute of Mental Health, depression is defined as a major depressive disorder. It is a common and serious mood disorder. It causes severe symptoms that affect how you feel, think, and handle daily activities, such as sleeping, eating, or working. To be diagnosed with depression, the symptoms must be present for at least two weeks.

Signs and Symptoms of Depression

If you have been experiencing some of the following signs and symptoms most of the day, nearly every day, for at least two weeks, you may be suffering from depression:

- Persistent sad, anxious, or "empty" mood
- Feelings of hopelessness, or pessimism
- Irritability
- Feelings of guilt, worthlessness, or helplessness
- Loss of interest or pleasure in hobbies and activities
- Decreased energy or fatigue
- Moving or talking more slowly
- Feeling restless or having trouble sitting still
- Difficulty concentrating, remembering, or making decisions
- Difficulty sleeping, early-morning awakening, or oversleeping
- Appetite and/or weight changes
- Thoughts of death or suicide, or suicide attempts
- Aches or pains, headaches, cramps, or digestive problems without a clear physical cause and/or that do not ease even with treatment. *Adapted from the National Institute of Mental Health.*

Reflect on these questions.

Have there been times that you felt intense sadness lasting more than a few days but not for two weeks or longer? _____

Have there been times when you didn't have the energy to get out of bed? _____

Have there been times when you withdrew from your friends? _____

Have there been times when you found it difficult to find joy in life? _____

Have there been times when you contemplated self-harm (such as suicide)?

"If you suffer from persistent feelings of low mood, irritability, disrupted sleep and appetite, withdrawal from friends, or thoughts of self-harm, you should speak to a professional, such as a family physician or mental health worker. Let someone know you're hurting."

Overcoming the Fear of Fear!

Depression clouded my judgment. Depression kept me feeling inadequate and unqualified. It kept me living in a dark place. Depression kept me frozen, scared to move, scared to step out, and scared to speak up.

Many people looked at me on the outside and thought I was okay, but I was dying on the inside. I was scared and silently screaming for someone to understand me, even though I could not even explain to them how I was feeling.

At times, it was hard keeping my kids encouraged, and it was hard for me to smile. It was very hard for me to deal with change, but most of all, I was feeling a loss of control. I always felt the need to control everything in my life. If it didn't go my way, I would feel anxious. Have you ever felt that way? I know I am not alone. I have come such a long way, and I am learning to surrender to God in every aspect of my life. I am not there yet, but one thing I know for sure is that I am growing. If you are still in the process of surrendering, let's touch and agree in the Holy Spirit that we will grow together and surrender all to Jesus.

I apologize and repent unto the Lord for delaying this task that he has asked me to do years ago. I apologize to myself for not believing in myself, and I apologize to those who remain locked up. I was in bondage as a result of my fears. I pray today that God will bring people who need to hear the message in this book. I pray for people to unlock every desire—every dream you may have. I pray you are set free as I am free. I had to reposition myself to do God's will. He was calling me. I had to change the way I thought of myself and let nothing interfere with the assignment that God called me to do.

I knew time was ticking and I had to do something. I noticed my depression and anxiety significantly decreased when I said yes to God, and when I accepted His assignment that He gave to me. God desires for us to have courage. Courage is defined as doing it even if you are afraid. I am learning in the middle of the fear and anxiety to just do it anyway.

What Is Stress and How Does It Affect Us?

According to Webster's Dictionary, stress is defined as a state of mental tension and worry caused by problems in your life and work, something that causes strong feelings of worry or anxiety, physical force, or pressure.

Stress, Triggers and How to Manage

Stress can cause symptoms of:

Anxiety

Depression

Insomnia

Asthma

Heart Disease

High Blood Pressure

Diabetes

Heart Disease

Alcoholism

Drug Addiction

Adapted from *Of Course You're Anxious* by Gayle Rosellini and Mark Worden

Since stress is so prevalent in many of our lives for whatever reason, I decided to take some time to research stress and its causes and then learn how to manage it. There are many different reasons why people experience stress. It can come from family, your job, or lack of finances (unable to provide for yourself and/or your family). During my research, I wanted to discover the root of the fear, anxiety, and stress. I also wanted to search for solutions for people to manage stress. These techniques are what can be applied to not only my life but to yours. I am a Christian and a woman of God, so I turn to the Bible and prayer as a way to relax and de-stress. I have learned how to stop, take deep breaths, be still in the moment, and not rush the process. It is important to allow your body to de-escalate from anxiety and stress for the moment. Symptoms of stress can vary from one person to another. My relationship with Jesus Christ and using my family as my support system truly helps me overcome my anxiety and stress.

Even though stress is a part of our lives, we do not have to allow it to consume us. If stress is left unmanaged it can affect your happiness, your health, and your ability to achieve your goals. With the right management techniques that work for you, you can regain control, clarity, focus and live a healthy and balanced life. (Greenberg 2016, 5)

How do you know if you are stressed? Think about how you have felt over the past two weeks. Check off the symptoms below that you have felt over the past two weeks or longer.

____Sleep disturbance

____Appetite Disturbance

____Smoking more

____Drinking more

____Increased Irritability and frustration

____Easy to anger

____Chest pain

____Breathing problems

____Tension in neck and shoulders

____Headaches

____Fatigue or lethargy

____Feeling edgy or anxious

____Feeling sad or tearful

____Problems with attention, concentration, memory

____General aches and pains

Triggers of Stress

1. Long hours on the job
2. Increased pressure at work
3. Living in a fast-paced society
4. Putting too much pressure on ourselves to have to succeed at everything that we do
5. Comparing ourselves, our lives, and our abilities to others
6. Social media is a huge trigger for stress

7. Relationships with others, particularly toxic ones

Signs and Symptoms of Stress

1. You may feel restless from lack of sleep.
2. You may have a loss of appetite and may not even want your favorite foods.
3. You may feel fatigued during the day from sleeping difficulties.
4. You may feel lonely, isolated, and may not want to talk to anyone.
5. It may be harder for you to concentrate and also hard for you to remember things.
6. You may become more irritable and more impatient with others.

Two Types of Stress

There are two types of stress: acute and chronic. Acute stress is a response to short-term stressors such as reciting a speech, speaking in public, going on a first date, or confronting others when there is a conflict.

The effects of chronic stress can affect you and your family and friends. "Over time, stress can affect your brain, heart, weight, resistance to disease, and even your genetic make-up."

"Stress impairs your brain cells' ability to transport and use glucose which is an important source of energy. Without enough glucose, your brain cells are less resilient and more vulnerable to damage" (Greenberg 2016, 23-24).

"Stress can also cause damage to your heart which could lead to hypertension, stroke, as well as a heart attack" (Greenberg 2016, 24).

I know that we have all experienced stress-eating. This will, of course, cause weight gain. Cortisol increases your appetite, which interferes with sleep and contributes to you choosing unhealthy food, especially when you're tired (Greenberg 2016, 24-25).

One thing my mom always told me was that stress can cause physical problems, and you could end up in the hospital. As a young teen, I didn't quite understand how that could happen but as I grew up and researched more on the effects of stress, she was right.

Stress can definitely affect your immune system.

Chronic stress has a strong tendency to weaken the immune system because it takes such a physical toll on your mind and body. "Your genetic makeup may make you less adaptable to change or more prone to anxiety" (The Stress-Proof Brain, p. 30). However, you

CAN overcome and take control of your mind and your situation.

Assessing Your Chronic Stressors

Let's take a look at the chronic stressors checklist

Place a checkmark next to all the stressors you experience regularly.

___fights with your partner

___financial stress, too much debt

___a partner, child, or parent with a mental or serious physical illness

___a high level of stress or demands at your job

___loneliness

___a lack of support or cooperation from others

___a noisy crowded, or uncomfortable living situation

___dissatisfaction with your weight or something else

The way I release stress is to first acknowledge it. I take time to pray and read some Bible Scriptures that encourage me. I also speak the affirmations over my life that I learned from Coach Stormy Wellington. You do not have to stay in that dark, chaotic stressful place. There is certainly a way out. Surround yourself with the right people. You may even have to change your inner circle of friends and possibly disconnect some people from your life. Let's slash these negatives feelings and emotions, one by one, and one day at a time.

Now let's take a look at fear, its definition, and how to manage it.

What are Fear, Anxiety, and Stress?

Fear is defined as an unpleasant emotion caused by the belief that someone or something is dangerous or likely to cause pain or a threat. *Anxiety* is defined as a feeling of worry, nervousness, or unease, typically about an imminent event or something with an uncertain outcome. *Stress* is defined as a state of mental or emotional strain or tension resulting from adverse or very demanding circumstances. We all experience fear. Some fear is healthy, especially when it warns us about a dangerous situation. Many times, we fear when there is turbulence on an airplane. I love flying but when there is turbulence, I have to admit that I get nervous and often nauseated. Anxiety, on the other hand, is what we experience when we think about what we could encounter or what might happen.

The purpose of this book is to let you know you are not alone. We all have felt fear, anxiety, and stress but please know that you are not alone. There are so many people who share the same feelings as you. In this book, I share my story, my children's story, and tips on how to manage it when it comes upon you.

Adapted from Overcoming the Fear of Fear

Do you know the top 10 Phobias?

10. Trypophobia- the fear of holes

9. Aerophobia- the fear of flying

8. Mysophobia- the fear of germs

7. Claustrophobia- the fear of small spaces

6. Astraphobia- the fear of thunder and lightning

5. Cynophobia- the fear of dogs

4. Agoraphobia- the fear of open or crowded spaces

3. Acrophobia-the fear of heights

2. Ophidiophobia- the fear of snakes

1. Arachnophobia- the fear of spiders

What Do Fear and Anxiety Feel like?

* Your heart beats very fast
* You breathe very fast
* Your muscles feel very weak
* You sweat a lot
* Your stomach churns or your bowels feel loose
* You find it hard to concentrate on anything else
* You feel dizzy
* You feel frozen on the spot
* You can't eat
* You have hot and cold sweats
* You get a dry mouth
* You get very tense muscles
* You get headaches

If you suffer from fear and anxiety, the first thing you want to do is identify the fear and anxiety. Take a moment and analyze where it is coming from and what are the triggers. This is not an easy process, and it can be very scary because it's going to cause you to dig deep into the roots of what may be causing anxiety. For me, anxiety was caused by fear. Also, you may be pushed out of your comfort zone in order to figure out what those triggers are because some unwanted memories may come back. But if you can just lean into those feelings for a moment to figure out the *why* so it does not overtake you, we can go ahead and address the *how* so you can know how to handle it.

Where Does Anxiety Come From?

Anxiety can be inherited, and it can be learned through your environment. Either way, at some point in your life, you will need to face it and find a way to manage it and decrease it as much as possible. (Watt & Stewart 2008).

"When adults get frightened, it's contagious, and children catch it too."-Anonymous

This quote tells me that our adult life is highly influenced and shaped by what we have learned during our childhood and adolescent years.

Think back when you were a child and had such symptoms as a racing heart, dizziness, shortness of breath, or nausea. Answer the following questions.

Did you panic? _____

Did you feel weak or light-headed? _____

Did you feel the need to lie down_____?

Did something scary happen as a result of these symptoms? _____

Now think about your parents and how they responded to your symptoms.

Did they understand how you were feeling? _____

Did they encourage you to stay home from school? _____

Did they give you special care? _____

Did your parents warn you about the dangers of your symptoms? _____

Did they take you to the doctor? _____

Were you given medication? _____

Adapted from *Overcoming the Fear of Fear*

Overcoming and Understanding Fear and Anxiety

So first, let's try to understand the fear.

It's very easy to ignore your fears. For years, I tried to ignore my fear and anxiety. I didn't want to face what was causing it. I later realized for me, I had to always be in control. The loss of control and the lack of not knowing what was going to happen next sparked anxiety inside of me. My anxiety peaked anytime there was a sudden change in life, in my schedule or anything I was not able to prepare for.

Now keep in mind when you begin to start unlocking the root of your fears, you're going to experience a range of emotions. You may be angry or you may be sad. Then you may become depressed. You may be afraid, resentful, or you may even get frustrated. As I mentioned earlier, during those moments while you are trying to overcome your fears, remain prayerful so that you can understand the cause of it and find a solution.

Once you experience a variety of emotions, find a way to release those emotions that are safe, non-threatening, and harmless. For example, you can engage in things that will give you peace of mind: you can write in a journal, take a walk, read a book, listen to music, dance, paint, cook, or sew. Any of these activities are a great diversion while you process those emotions.

I like to speak affirmations over my life to give me the courage I need and to help me get over my fears.

Here is an affirmation I would like to share with you. In March of 2016, I learned this affirmation from Coach Stormy Wellington, and I have taught it to both of my children.

I will hear the voice

Of the holy spirit within

I will lead and not follow

I will create and not destroy

I am a force for good

I defy the odds

I set new standards

I am the head and not the tail

I am above and not beneath

I am the lender and not the borrower

I am loved by God

I am chosen by GOD

I am protected by GOD

No weapon formed against me shall prosper

And every tongue that rises against me in judgment
shall be condemned

It is my season

It's my turn

I am happy

I am healthy

I am humble

I am wealthy

I am strong

I AM A CHAMPION!!!

Learn Ways to Deescalate When You Are Experiencing Fear and Anxiety

Here are a few suggestions: Choose what is safe and what works best for you. You can exercise, learn relaxation techniques, eat healthy, avoid alcohol or drink in moderation, find a therapist who you are comfortable talking with, and find support groups so you are not alone. Activate your faith and spirituality to give you strength, comfort, and hope.

Once you address and identify the fear, you can start doing the work to let go of the fears. I find when fear is no longer a secret, the drive to get rid of it motivates you to eliminate it.

You CAN overcome anxiety. You do not have to live in a state of constant fear. However, this change will not happen overnight but with time, patience, and lots of support, you will get there. Find out what works best for you. At some point, as I have learned, you will get tired of being afraid and running away. You will face your fears head-on.

Chapter 4

The BREAKTHROUGH

In many ways, I have self-sabotaged in lots of areas in my life. Now that I am aware of the things that have been blocking me, I have made the decision that I will fight every day to never allow fear to rule and control my life.

I used to think I was alone because no one was talking about anxious feelings, depression, and panic attacks. There are so many things that cause one to have fear and anxiety. Even though I spoke in the church as a child, I still have anxiety when it comes to speaking in public. Now I don't mind praying in public but speaking in public on a certain topic scares me. However, I know I must do it anyway. I pray and ask God to keep me focused on Him. I know for sure while feeling fearful and anxious, God is there when I call on Him. Someone asked me a great question. What do you do when the anxious feeling comes back? My reply is that you become aware the feeling is there, pray to God for strength, and deescalate by taking deep breaths. Take a walk, write in your journal, dance, or do whatever makes you happy and gives you peace. Do not be afraid of those feelings of anxiety because you know this too shall pass. When I surrendered to God and operated in my purpose, I no longer cared that the anxiety was there. I know God has my back, so I am going to keep operating in my purpose and keep pushing to overcome my anxieties.

At some point, it was time to anoint me, my family, and my home with anointing oil. I had to fast and pray and lay hands on myself. We are always battling something. Have you ever heard a preacher say, "You have just come out of a storm," "You are currently in a storm," or "You are about to go through a storm"?

"And being in Bethany in the house of Simon the leper as He sat at the table, a woman came having an alabaster box of very costly oil of spikenard. She broke the flask and poured it on His head." - Mark 14:3

When I think of the song "Alabaster Box" by CeCe Winans, I see myself carrying the anointing oil, dancing at the feet of Jesus and not having a care in the world.

Social Media and Anxiety

Social media is the number one source of anxiety because everyone is painting this perfect picture of life. People want to see realness. As I study and research why so many people are fearful, anxious, stressed and depressed, I believe social media plays a huge part. I also believe the mind plays a huge part.

Have you heard of FOMO? It stands for the Fear of Missing Out. This is a huge trigger for anxiety. For example, there may be pictures of a gathering where the user was not invited to attend events and parties. They may not have been able to attend due to work/family schedule. However, the lack of attending causes sadness, eventually leading to low self-esteem.

Social media platforms can greatly affect your mental health. It has become an anxiety-provoking factor. Social media such as Facebook and Instagram can increase people's stress levels. It causes anxiety and affects people's self-esteem and quality of sleep in a negative way.

According to the Anxiety and Depression Association of America, social media testing has found that using too much of the internet can cause depression, ADHD, impulsive disorder, problems with mental functioning, paranoia, and loneliness. I researched the causes of social media's negative effects on people.

According to Anxiety.org, there is a "compare and despair" factor. This is when we see the perfect couples, perfect family pictures, and vacations all over the world. We then compare that to our lives or the fact we have not traveled to those places with our own families. I have been guilty at times of thinking I was not doing enough for my children and that I wasn't giving them enough experiences as their friends had. I realized the first thing my children wanted from my husband and me was our time. They don't care if it is at home or Disney World. Time equals love to them. I completely understand why comparison is the thief of joy! On Facebook, many tend to get caught up in the number of likes on a particular post or picture, which can cause anxiety, despair, and depression.

There has to be a balance. You should decrease the amount of time you spend on social media scrolling and comparing your life to others. Improper use of social media can harm your mental health. If you are using it to better yourself or if you are in a particular group where you are growing and learning, then that is great. However, if it is causing you to feel bad about yourself and your family, you need to set limits and stick to them. Take a break, regroup, and get to the source of why you are feeling this way so social media can be of value to you versus a mental/emotional hindrance.

When Anxiety Becomes a Problem!

Some anxiety is normal and not always bad. However, when it becomes severe and happens frequently, it can result in panic attacks, fear, and discomfort. It can also be debilitating. It can prevent you from moving forward or even completing a project or assignment that God has given you. This is what happened to me. Fear and anxiety caused me to procrastinate, therefore I delayed many of the assignments God had for me.

What Kinds of Situations Make You Anxious?

(Adapted from *Overcoming the Fear of Fear*)

Please check the situations that apply to you.

_____Speaking in public

_____Participating in groups

_____Walking upstairs or hills

_____Darkness

_____Being Alone

_____Getting really angry

_____Being in closed spaces (such as elevators or cars with the windows rolled up)

How do you feel when you're anxious?

Please check the situations that apply to you

_____Heart racing or fluttering

_____Rapid breathing

_____Head aching

_____Choking or suffocating

_____Chest pains

_____Sweating

_____Dizziness

_____Other sensations

Many times, when anxiety becomes out of control, a panic attack may follow. According to Wikipedia, panic attacks are sudden periods of intense fear that may include palpitations, sweating, shaking, shortness of breath, numbness, or a feeling that something bad is going to happen. The maximum degree of symptoms occurs within minutes. Typically, they last for about 30 minutes, but the duration can vary from seconds to hours. There may be a fear of losing control and chest pain. Panic attacks are not typically dangerous physically.

When fear and anxiety come, just know because you are a child of God and God has His hand on you, it will not have authority over you. God is so amazing that things you may be fearful of or that may cause anxiety, God would never even have those issues cross your path. He knows what you can handle. He knows what He wants you to accomplish. God will guide you along the way if you just trust in Him and know that He is in total control.

I'm so thankful that God remembered me even when I was running away from Him. I'm so thankful that God kept His hands on me, even during times I turned my back on Him because I was mad my life was not going the way I thought it should. It was not going the way I had planned. I thank God for giving me another chance to fulfill His purpose in my life while I was running away from Him and from my calling. I know God was right there with me. He was right by my side the entire time. Sometimes when bad things happen to me, I don't always handle it the way I believe God wants me to. I understand bad things happen all the time to different people, but I want to do a better job of handling things as it happens to me, especially when I feel I am not in control, or when it is hard to find a solution. I have learned I don't have control over how certain situations will go.

I am so thankful that the divorce I experienced after 10 years of marriage didn't take me under. I'm so thankful after knowing of my daughter's liver condition that it didn't take me under. I'm thankful that my son is an overcomer and he is growing up to be a wonderful young man. I'm thankful that God gave me another chance to get married to my high school sweetheart — the love of my life — who has been there for me and my children. I'm thankful I was able to keep and maintain hope and not fall into despair after my divorce. For three years, I was single and then God blessed me with my amazing husband Derrick. He has truly loved, supported, and protected me and our children. I am so grateful for my support system and my parents who were right there with me through it all. I am writing this book to encourage you to not give up. Keep going and keep moving forward. Stay connected to the right people. Keep your circle small. Do your best to attend gatherings and conferences that are designed to uplift you.

I can tell you the day I decided to write this book, I did not know who would want to buy it. However, it didn't matter. All I wanted to do was fulfill God's purpose to get the book out because God told me to do it years ago. However, due to my fears, anxieties, and insecurities, and because I was still dealing with my own inner battles, I felt inadequate. I was reminded of a poem by Marion Williamson called "Our Deepest Fear".

Our Deepest Fear!

"Our deepest fear is not that we are inadequate. Our deepest fear is that we are powerful beyond measure. It is our light, not our darkness, that most frightens us. Your playing small does not serve the world. There is nothing enlightened about shrinking so that other people won't feel insecure around you. We are all meant to shine as children do. It's not just in some of us; it is in everyone. And as we let our own lights shine, we unconsciously give other people permission to do the same. As we are liberated from our own fear, our presence automatically liberates others." - Marianne Williamson

My mother taught me a poem called "Heaven's Grocery Store" when I was a little girl. I love this poem because it reminds me that God wants us to live in peace and not worry about anything.

"I was walking down life's highway a long time ago. I saw a sign that read, Heavens Grocery Store. As I got a little closer, the doors came open wide. As I came to myself, I was standing inside. Angels were standing everywhere. First, I got some patience, love was in the same row, further down was understanding, and you need that everywhere you go. I stopped to get some strength and courage to help me run this race. Then I remembered that I needed some grace. Peace and Joy were plentiful, and they were on the last shelf. Songs and praises were hanging near, so I just helped myself. Then I said to the angel, how much do I owe, he just smiled and said, take them everywhere you go. Again, I smiled at him and said now how much do I really owe? He just smiled at me and said, my child, Jesus paid your bills a long time ago."

Scriptures that Speak

"For I am persuaded, that neither death, nor life, nor angels, nor principalities, nor powers, nor things present, nor things to come, nor height, nor depth, nor any other creature, shall be able to separate us from the love of God, which is in Christ Jesus our Lord." (King James Version, Romans 8:38-39).

The Bible says to let nothing separate you from the love of God. If you are living a life full of fear, anxiety, insecurities, and depression, give it over to Jesus. Fight as hard as you can to keep saying "Yes." Say yes to God. Keep talking to God and keep pouring your heart out to him. I promise you, at some point, your breakthrough will come. You are going to fulfill every assignment that God has for you. You are going to walk in so much boldness when you say yes to God. Once you release some of the fear and anxiety, it still may be there just a little, but that's okay. That holy boldness will rise up inside of you and you will set so many captives free in the midst of all that you're going through. Your freedom and breakthrough are going to break so many people's chains so they too can be free. God will be pleased, and you will feel so amazing because you said yes!

Ever since I was a child, I knew I was different. I knew I was cut from a different piece of cloth. I knew I was anointed for greatness. I knew it. Anxiety is a beast. Depression is a beast. If you let it overrule your life, it will STOP you from moving forward. Overcome your fear, answer the call, and walk in your purpose!

Fear and anxiety have gripped you for so long. For some of you reading this, it has been months, but for many of you, it has been years of being trapped in bondage. There comes a time when you have to stop watching others win. You must accomplish your goals and win for yourself and your family! Why? Others are waiting on your story, your breakthrough, and your release so that they too can be free! You are powerful! You have what it takes! It's in you but you must make a DECISION to link up with those who are going where you want to go! You must be aligned with the right people in your life. I pray that this book encourages and pushes you into greatness. You deserve every good thing that comes your way. Keep pushing and know that God, and the people He has placed and aligned in your life, will help you get to YOUR next level!

Chapter 5

God's Love

God loves you so much that you came across this very book. This is your time and you have to believe that God's hand is on you and has always been on you. In spite of all the pain that you have gone through, the trials and tribulations, afflictions, neglect, and emotional abuse, God still loves you.

John 15:9-12. says,

As the Father has loved me, so have I loved you. Now remain in my love. If you keep my commands, you will remain in my love, just as I have kept my Father's commands and remain in His love. I have told you this so that my joy may be in you and that your joy may be complete. My command is this: Love each other as I have loved you. (New International Version).

This Scripture speaks to me because it reminds me that whoever has hurt me in the past, let it go and keep love in my heart. You don't have to go back to that person or to that situation, but you don't want to have bitterness ruling your heart. You want God's love and joy to remain full in you so you can get to your next blessing instead of allowing the pains of your past to hinder you from moving forward.

Scriptures That Speak

Take a moment and reflect on each Scripture. Write down what it means to you.

*James 1:2-4 20 New King James Version (NKJV)

My brethren, count it all joy when you fall into various trials, knowing that the testing of your faith produces patience. But let patience have its perfect work, that you may be perfect and complete, lacking nothing.

_____

_____

_____

_____

_____

_____

_____

Acts 2:17-20 New King James Version (NKJV)

And it shall come to pass in the last days, says God,

That I will pour out of My Spirit on all flesh;

Your sons and your daughters shall prophesy,

Your young men shall see visions,

Your old men shall dream dreams.

And on My menservants and on My maidservants

I will pour out My Spirit in those days;

And they shall prophesy.

I will show wonders in heaven above

And signs in the earth beneath:

Blood and fire and vapor of smoke.

The sun shall be turned into darkness,

And the moon into blood,

Before the coming of the great and awesome day of the LORD.

_____

_____

_____

_____

_____

This Scripture really blesses me and gives me hope for the world because God is ready and willing to pour out His Spirit on us. He's ready and willing to accept His children with open arms but we all know we have free will. God is not going to force you to do anything. Whenever you call on the name of the Lord, as the Word says, you will be saved. When you are dealing with struggles, anxieties, depression, insecurities and fear, call on the name of the Lord because he has His hand on you.

Surrendering It All

What does it truly mean to surrender? What does it mean to surrender everything to God?

It's scary when you think of the word surrender because you know there is something or someone that you may need to give up or release back to God. There is a habit you know you will have to work on breaking. For me, surrendering to God means letting go of control. I think the biggest issue in my life is having a sense of independence and being in control of everything. When I find that I have to be dependent on others, I sometimes feel helpless. However, I had to learn that I can't control my husband; I can't even control my children because they have their own mind, and I can't control circumstances in life or the way I think life is supposed to go. Now I do believe we can alter or change something in our lives, but some things are truly out of your control. This reminds me of a special prayer my mom taught me when I was a teenager.

Serenity Prayer

God, grant me the *Serenity*, to accept the things I cannot change, the *Courage* to change the things I can, and the *Wisdom* to know the difference.

Let Go of Your Idols

Some people worship idols and put these idols before God. Those things/idols definitely have to be surrendered to God and released from your life. The more I reflect on my life as I write this book, it seems that my idol was worry, fear, and the need to always be in control. When I was in deep thought, I was reminded fear is the opposite of faith, and I had been living a life of doubt for so long, but no more. As I write this book, I am taking a moment to really dig deep into my own soul. I have given myself permission to break out of the mental bond that I believe I put myself in and the box I allowed others to put me in too. There were definitely some painful moments in my life and some hurtful things that people have said to me. I allowed it to stay with me way too long. God never said those things about me. In Jeremiah 29:11 God reminded me, "I know the plans that I have for you says the Lord, plans to prosper you and not to harm you to give you a future and a hope." God told me this a long time ago, but when we venture off away from God and conform to the things of the world rather than the things of God, we lose sight of all that God has for us. I also remember the Prayer of Jabez that says, "I will bless you indeed, and I will enlarge your territory, I will keep my hand upon you that you may not cause pain."

I think about all the times God spoke to me and all the deep conversations/supernatural experiences I've had with God throughout my life. But somewhere along the way when a curveball came, it shocked me and it rocked me, and it caused me to experience the doubt. As a result, fear took over.

I know many of you have experienced the fear of not being in control. I pray that my story blesses you and reassures you that you are not alone. I found after talking to different people, particularly women, so many of us have hidden fears, anxieties, and insecurities. The problem of not talking about it is because we think we are not going to be understood or we are afraid of being judged. However, when women come together and are transparent, we find we are on one accord, and we find we have more in common than what we thought.

I'm reminded of the Scripture in 1st Corinthians 2:9-10, "But as it is written, Eye hath not seen, nor ear heard, neither have entered into the heart of man the things which God has prepared for them that love him, but God had revealed them to us by his Spirit: for the Spirit searcheth all things yea, the deep things of God." (King James Version)

Scriptures That Speak

Ephesians 4:17-24

The New Man

This I say, therefore, and testify in the Lord, that you should no longer walk as the rest of the Gentiles walk, in the futility of their mind, having their understanding darkened, being alienated from the life of God, because of the ignorance that is in them, because of the blindness of their heart; who, being past feeling, have given themselves over to lewdness, to work all uncleanness with greediness.

But you have not so learned Christ, if indeed you have heard Him and have been taught by Him, as the truth is in Jesus: that you put off, concerning your former conduct, the old man which grows corrupt according to the deceitful lusts, and be renewed in the spirit of your mind, and that you put on the new man which was created according to God, in true righteousness and holiness. (New King James Version).

Scriptures That Speak

Isaiah 55:3

Give ear and come to me, listen that you may live. I will make an everlasting covenant with you, my faithful love promised to David. (New International Version).

Words of Wisdom from God Directly Imparted into Me

1. God said I have chosen you, but you must accept your calling because many are called but few are chosen.
2. Don't lose focus. Stay connected to me.
3. It's hard to have faith and fear at the same time.
4. Stop telling others what I have told you in secret. Let it manifest in your mind and heart first. I will bring it to pass.
5. I am trying to get you ready for something greater.
6. Surrender and make yourself totally available to Me.

March 25th, 2001, God said this is a new beginning for you. That is why the number eight is so significant. Eight in the Bible means a new beginning. God reminded me way back in 2001 that my relationship with God, myself, my family, and my dance ministry were all a new beginning. God continues to remind me that He is always doing a new thing in me.

Scriptures That Speak

Psalm 126:5-6

Those who sow in tears will reap songs of joy. Those who go out weeping and carrying seeds to sow will return with songs of joy, carrying sheaves with them. (New International Version).

Sheaves are defined as bundles of cereal plants, wheat rye, a harvest after a time of sowing and reaping. So as you sow, get ready for the abundance and overflow of God's blessings.

Scriptures That Speak

Luke 1:45

Blessed is she who has believed that the Lord would fulfill his promises to her. (New International Version)

Scriptures That Speak

Joshua 24:15

But if serving the Lord seems undesirable to you, then choose for yourselves this day whom you will serve, whether the gods of your ancestors served beyond the Euphrates, or the gods of the Amorites, in whose land you are living. But as for me and my household, we will serve the Lord. (New International Version).

Blaming Yourself and or Others

Blaming can also cause a great deal of stress and anxiety. Blame can eventually turn into guilt. Guilt can cause you to worry for a very long time and to feel a range of emotions that can be very debilitating. You may experience sadness, anger, and depression.

Self-Love

We all need to have self-love, true peace, true love, and true happiness. It is so important that you get to know the true you. That will take lots of time, prayer, patience and self-discovery.

On the lines below, take a moment and write down at least three things you love about yourself. Think about positive thoughts that you can tell yourself every day. When you think positively about yourself and your situation, no matter how bad it is, your anxieties and fears will de-escalate and subside.

_____

_____

_____

_____

_____

_____

_____

_____

_____

_____

_____

_____

I read in *Think and Grow Rich* that you become what you think about. Whatever you plant in your mind, it will produce. There is also a Scripture in the Bible in Proverbs 23:7 and it says, "For as he thinks in his heart, so is he." (NKJV). Sometimes when we are alone, we tend to think about problems and circumstances we are facing in our lives. I have found that sometimes the hardest thing for a lot of people is being alone. You can be alone but not necessarily feel lonely. You can be alone and enjoy that time with yourself just doing the things you love to do or going places you love to go. That seems to be hard for a lot of people. Sometimes being alone forces you to think about your current situation and the things you have done in your past. However, if you take that time to face yourself and your inadequacies and insecurities, you will find that self-love will evolve. And once self-love evolves, you will develop healthy relationships with other people. When you treat yourself well, then you teach other people how to treat you! Know who you are in God and see yourself how God sees you.

Imaginations

Sometimes our imaginations can cause fear, stress, and anxiety.

When we stress or obsess over the "what ifs," we create a downward spiral for ourselves. I have been guilty of filling my mind with what if this happens and what if that happens. This type of thinking did nothing for me but made me feel worse and stressed out. My advice is to guard your thoughts and be cautious about making assumptions. This reminds me of the Scripture in II Corinthians 10:4-5, "For the weapons of our warfare are not carnal, but mighty through God to the pulling down of strongholds. Casting down imaginations, and every high thing that exalteth itself against the knowledge of God, and bringing in captivity every thought to the obedience of Christ."

A Breaking Point

When I began this journey writing my book, I had no idea I was going to go through spiritual warfare throughout this journey and back to back incidents. However, it was nothing that overtook me where I couldn't complete this book. God delivered me out all of them. There are times along this journey that I wanted to stop writing this book. It seemed as though all hell broke loose. My father was sick for one week. He was suffering from a bad stomachache and ended up having to go to the emergency room to get fluids back in his body. My daughter woke up one morning with a slight fever and because of her condition, a fever is extremely alarming, and it worried me. Then, I accidentally hit my foot on the door of my bedroom and injured my toe. It was one thing after another.

I knew by me writing this book, the enemy was mad and tried to slow me down. I knew I was just being tested, but this was the first time I did not let it stop me or slow me down. I didn't allow fear, anxiety, or worry to grip my mind. My flesh wanted to lean in and give in to the fear and anxiety, but the Spirit of the Lord kept telling me to keep going, to trust him and not to worry because he had my parents and family taken care of and covered under the blood of Jesus.

I have come to understand there is warfare attached to my assignment of writing this book. It didn't come easy, nor did it flow just the way I wanted it to. I had to go through a few bumps in the road on the way to completion of this book. I couldn't allow the enemy to take over what God has anointed. The Word of God says, "touch not my anointed and do my prophets no harm," so I knew God had me covered!

What is so incredible about this journey is that as I'm writing about fear and anxiety, I was actually put to the test various times. When unexpected incidents happened, my first reaction was panic, fear, shock, and wanting to cry. I believe a lot comes from a loss of control. For the most part, when the incidents were happening back to back, I took it all in stride; but one summer when my dog ran away, I really thought I had lost her. As you can imagine, fear and anxiety gripped me. As soon as she took off, I chased her down the street in my neighborhood, then lost sight of her, but eventually found her in the backyard of someone's home not too far from mine. I was out of breath and shaking. I broke down and was extremely emotional. I was overwhelmed yet relieved and proud of myself for acting and not panicking. I laid down for a moment and just cried. Mostly, my tears were out of gratefulness but also out of fear of what could have happened. At that moment, I realized how remarkable my instinct kicked in gear. I was proud of myself and my ability to think on my feet and not panic. I immediately ran with such agility and determination to get my dog, and I didn't care at that moment if I was going to encounter other dogs in my neighborhood. I just knew I had to find Disney. This is one example of how I pushed past my fears and did not allow my anxiety to cause me to panic.

Feeling a Loss of Control

I remember when my Dad called me to let me know he had been having stomach pain that whole week. He mentioned getting blood work done to see what was going on. My parents don't always share things with me because of their fear that I'm going to worry. In most circumstances, if not all, they are right. But this time when he told me, I pretty much held it together. I felt like I couldn't break down. I did not like the fact that they were over 1,000 miles away knowing I couldn't get to him, but I still remained strong. However, there was also a small part of me that felt like maybe I should stop writing this book. It almost seemed as if the more I pushed through to write my story, the more opposition came my way. When my dad also told me he ended up having to go to the emergency room to receive fluids because he was very dehydrated, it was a lot for me to handle.

I had to prove to myself that I was working on me. I was working on handling things in a totally different way than what I was accustomed to. I'm not saying I completely have it all together, but I will say I'm definitely better than what I used to be.

Ways to Manage Stress

Relax by remaining still, having quiet time, and taking deep breaths. Taking the time to breathe may sound like it's unnecessary, but this is a major step to calming down. Taking slow and long breaths can decrease physical aches and pains as well. Deep breathing can help in the relief of anxieties too. Learning how to breathe properly will help you relax your body and mind. When you are at home, you can take some time to find a quiet space, light a candle, read a good book, and relax. Sometimes you just need time to allow the body and mind to calm down.

Another way to relax is to get some sleep. Sleep is something I tend to run from. I love being active, but it is important to know when to stop and rest. I am learning the importance of shutting some things down at night, watching a good movie, enjoying family time, reading a good book, reading my Bible, listening to some relaxing sleep music, and then drifting off to sleep. When I do that, I have to honestly say I wake up more refreshed and ready to face the next day.

Triggers

Take some time to identify the times of the day when you feel the emotional tension of stress. Stress can come from being in a certain place. Stress can come from hearing a certain type of music depending on the lyrics and even the sound. Stress can come from being around a person or group of people. Stress can also come from being in a certain place that is not lining up with your spirit or your emotion. Get a journal and start taking note of those stressful incidents. When those stressful moments arise, practice taking deep breaths immediately. I have always been told that it takes 21 days to create a habit. Once I intentionally dug deep and recognized where my stress was coming from, I knew what I could do to help myself get through it. I began my calming techniques such as praying, deep breathing, being still, and allowing myself to become calm.

It is imperative that when the stressful and anxious feeling arises, quickly start with the relaxation techniques so it doesn't escalate. De-escalation is the goal, so remember to do what works best for you.

Scriptures that Speak

Isaiah 59:1

"Behold, the LORD's hand is not shortened, that it cannot save; neither his ear heavy, that it cannot hear." (King James Version).

Scriptures that Speak

Matthew 11: 28 - 30

"Come to me, all you who are weary and burdened, and I will give you rest. Take my yoke upon you and learn from me, for I am gentle and humble in heart, and you will find rest for your souls. For my yoke is easy and my burden is light." (New International Version).

Confession

I have a fear of making mistakes. I put pressure on myself to make the right decision especially when it involves my children. I know that many moms feel this way. I am realizing that the journey to success may be stressful but in the end, everything will be all right and God will come through.

Here are some of my favorite quotes that have encouraged me in my life:

If you're walking down the right path and willing to keep walking eventually you'll make progress. -Barack Obama

If you fail to plan, you're planning to fail. -Benjamin Franklin

If everyone is moving forward together then success takes care of itself. -Henry Ford

Hard days are the best days because that's where champions are made. So if you push through the hard days, you can get through anything. -Gabby Douglas

If it has been done then it can be done -Lenika Scott Millionaire Mom

I have engaged in the vision that is bigger than myself so that nothing or no one can get in the way. -Stormy Wellington

Life isn't about waiting for the storm to pass... it's about learning to dance in the rain! Let's Dance!- Tonya Joyner Scott

You were born to win, but to be a winner, you must plan to win, prepare to win, and expect to win!

-Zig Ziglar

You may need to restructure some things, but when it's all over, you will step into the next dimension.- Bishop T.D. Jakes

Your destiny is determined by your decisions. - Tony Robbins

You will pay now, or you will pay later, but either way, you will pay. - Johnny DiBartolo, Jr., my dad

Everything is possible for him who believes. -Mark 9:23

Learn to be happy with what you have while you pursue all that you want. -Jim Rohn

The path to success is to take massive, determined action. - Tony Robbins

The choice to be excellent begins with aligning your thoughts and words with the intention to require more from yourself. -Oprah Winfrey

Unless you change who you are, you will always have what you got. -Jim Rohn

Whenever you are trying to grow, always connect with those who are on a higher level than you so that you can grow higher too. -Pastor Johnny DiBartolo,III, my brother

God may not come when you want Him, but He is always on time. If you can trust God for one thing, then trust God for everything. -Eva DiBartolo, my mom

Final Thought!

There comes a time in your life that you must decide if you will stay stuck in the same place you have been in for months or even years, or if you will decide to rise up and step out on faith to achieve the goals you have set for yourself. You see, fear is that strong feeling that causes many people to not reach their fullest potential. It is more painful to stay frozen and stuck in one place than it is to blossom. Although it can be very scary to step out in faith, there is also peace and freedom as you step. You do not have to know it all, but you must have the passion to fuel where you are going. I know for sure that as you step out on faith, God will send the right people to help you on your journey. Remember to be conscious and aware of alignment. Divine connection is everything!

You must look inside yourself and ask what is it you feel you are really afraid of. It also helps to share that fear with one or two friends or family members who you can trust. I have found that once you put it out there, you will find ways to cope and still move on because you now have a support system. The fear and anxiety will diminish, or it will go away completely.

I strongly believe you need courage in order to accomplish your daily goals to see the results you are seeking. I am at the point in my life of addressing and facing my fears one by one! It may not happen all at once, but it's okay because I am always learning and growing. As I go through life, I am becoming aware and courageous. Courage does not just happen accidentally. You have to have courage and face your fears head-on. You must change your mindset and speak positive encouraging words in your mind and your heart on a daily basis. It has to be embedded in you so you can uproot all of your fears, anxieties, negativity, past hurts, mistakes, and adopt a brand new mind which leads you to a new way of seeing the world. You should decide to not only have faith but to really believe you will push past it. James 2:17 says that faith without works is dead! You cannot just have faith and wish for success. You must take action and the necessary steps to achieve your goals. It will require you to hear God's voice and move when He says to move! Don't worry about making a mistake. I have already shared that one of my biggest fears was making the wrong decision! This is paralyzing because it keeps you stuck and afraid to move! I pray now that you are becoming free. I am becoming free as I write this book. I took a leap of faith to write this book. I am enjoying the journey, but at times it is painful because I am doing internal work as well! Know that God's got you! When you are aligned, the right people will come your way to help take you to your next level.

Steve Harvey talked about making the decision to jump. He said jumping is scary. When you first jump, your parachute will not open right away, and at times it will feel like it's an uncontrollable tumble. But if you never jump, your parachute will never open. You will be safe, but you will carry a closed parachute on your back full of skills and gifts. He added that if you don't jump, you will never get hurt but you will also never soar, and you will never know what you could have accomplished.

I learned we cannot control what happens in our lives; we control how we respond to it. When we do not respond to it correctly, we become stressed. Tony Robbins said, "It is not necessarily the conditions of our lives but the decisions we make in our lives." Robbins spoke on overcoming depression and anxiety. We have a choice. We choose how we handle what happens to us, and it is a decision. You have to decide what you focus on because that will determine how you respond to a situation. You have to be fully aware of your thoughts and make a conscious effort in your decision. What you focus on, you will manifest. You also want to be careful not to prejudge/judge others based on your perception. Sometimes we can come up with an idea of how a person feels about us and many times we are wrong. Assumptions can also lead to stress and anxiety because we put the wrong thought in our minds.

That moment when you know you've been set free and that shift that I've been speaking about is happening—it all starts in the mind! I pray each of you break free from whatever is holding you back!

Whom the Son sets free is free indeed! I remember telling God that I repent for not operating fully in my calling.

I repent for not believing in the fullness of His power.

I repent for not believing in myself and all that God placed in me.

I repent for delaying and ignoring so many of the assignments that God asked me to do.

I now operate out of faith and abundance. Even if I am afraid, I am learning to Do It Anyway! I believe in God's Word. He said His yoke is easy and His burden light. So that tells me I don't need to worry or struggle. You got this Lord!!! The battle is not mine, it's truly the Lord's! At that moment, I realized my anxiety and stress were reduced significantly. When that feeling arises, I am now aware of it and I cast it down in the name of Jesus.

We truly can have all that our heart desires for ourselves and our family! Supernaturally, we already have it all. We must now take the necessary steps to achieve those goals. It is imperative that you surround yourself with positive people-- those who are aligned with you and assigned to you so that you can break free and soar in every aspect of your life!

Resources

King James Version Bible

MentalHealth.org

T.D. Jakes Motivation- "You Are Not Powerless"

Stormy Wellington- Affirmation

Marianne Williamson- "Our Deepest Fear" Poem

Of Course You're Anxious (1990) Gayle Rosellini & Mark Worden

Overcoming the Fear of Fear (2008) by Margo C. Watt, Ph.D. and Sherry H. Stewart, Ph.D.

The Stress-Proof Brain (2016) by Melanie Greenberg, Ph.D.

About Wynette

Wynette Turner was born and raised in New Orleans, Louisiana. She attended Wesleyan College in Macon, Georgia and received a bachelor's degree in psychology. She also attended Delta State University in Cleveland, Mississippi where she received her Master of Education in School Counseling. She is happily married to her high school sweetheart, Derrick Turner. They have two beautiful children: a son 13 and a daughter 8. Wynette is a full-time elementary school counselor where she serves pre-K through 5th-grade pupils. She loves kids and desires to continue helping them to believe in themselves and have high self-esteem. She is a part-time entrepreneur and Life Changer for Total Life Changes, as well as the co-owner with her husband of a family enterprise T-shirt and designs company. She is now an author of her first book *Break Free and Soar: Letting Go of Fear, Anxiety, and Depression*. This book project is one of her biggest accomplishments. She is on a mission to help others become the best version of themselves while releasing their fears and anxieties. Wynette has a true desire to please God and has a heart to serve others. Her life, her battles, and her triumphs have molded her into the strong woman she is today. She is known to many as a motivator and inspiration. She knows that no weapon formed against her will prosper. She lives by Jeremiah 29:11- "For I know the thoughts that I think toward you, says the Lord, thoughts of peace and not of evil, to give you a future and a hope."

Follow Wynette on
Facebook: Wynette Turner, Bling with Wynette
and Instagram @clarkwynette

Visit her T-shirt website at
www.afamilyenterprise.com

and her health and wellness website at
www.tealadywynette.com

Made in the USA
San Bernardino, CA
16 June 2020